Oregon
The Beaver State

Marcia Amidon Lusted

PowerKiDS
press.

New York

Published in 2010 by The Rosen Publishing Group, Inc.
29 East 21st Street, New York, NY 10010

First Edition

Editor: Nicole Pristash
Book Layout: Julio Gil
Book Design: Greg Tucker
Photo Researcher: Jessica Gerweck

Photo Credits: Cover © Tim McGuire/Corbis; pp. 5, 13, 17, 22 (tree, flower, flag front and back) Shutterstock.com; pp. 7, 9, 22 (Chief Joseph) MPI/Getty Images; p. 11 © Craig Tuttle/Corbis; p. 15 © Donald Higgs/age fotostock; p. 19 Ron and Patty Thomas/Getty Images; p. 22 (beaver) © www.iStockphoto.com/kawisign; p. 22 (bird) © www.iStockphoto.com/Noah Strycker; p. 22 (Beverly Cleary) Terry Smith/Time Life Pictures/Getty Images; p. 22 (Matt Groening) Alberto E. Rodriguez/ Getty Images.

Library of Congress Cataloging-in-Publication Data

Lusted, Marcia Amidon.
    Oregon : the Beaver State / Marcia Amidon Lusted. — 1st ed.
        p. cm. — (Our amazing states)
    Includes index.
    ISBN 978-1-4358-9346-7 (library binding) — ISBN 978-1-4358-9786-1 (pbk.) — ISBN 978-1-4358-9787-8 (6-pack)
    1. Oregon—Juvenile literature. I. Title.
    F876.3.L87 2010
    979.5—dc22
                                                2009025511

Manufactured in the United States of America

CPSIA Compliance Information: Batch #WW10PK: For Further Information contact Rosen Publishing, New York, New York at 1-800-237-9932

Contents

Oregon the Beautiful

In which state can you see sea lions, visit the deepest lake in the United States, or walk to a waterfall? **Pioneers** in covered wagons once traveled across the country to get to this state. Today, **logging** trucks travel its roads. Did you guess which state it is? It is Oregon!

Oregon is found in the northwestern part of the United States. Its western edge touches the Pacific Ocean. Oregon lies between Washington, which is north of the state, and California, which is south.

Oregon may be best known for logging and lumber. However, Oregon is also known for its clean air and beautiful scenery. Many people think it is a wonderful place to live.

Oregon is known for its natural beauty. Here you can see Ecola State Park, on Oregon's coast, which offers great views of the Pacific Ocean.

Exploring Oregon

The first people to live in the area now known as Oregon lived there at least 13,000 years ago. Later, more than 100 different **tribes**, such as the Chinook, Nez Perce, and Shasta, made it their home.

In 1805, the **explorers** Meriwether Lewis and William Clark built a fort and spent the winter on the coast of Oregon. Clark described it as wet and cold. However, Lewis and Clark reported that Oregon was a good place for fur trading. During this time, many people used animal furs to make top hats and other clothing. When word got out that Oregon would be a good place to trade, fur trappers came to Oregon. These people were some of the first settlers in the area.

This painting shows explorers Meriwether Lewis and William Clark at the mouth of the Columbia River, on the coast of Oregon, in 1805.

The Oregon Trail

Starting in the early 1840s, many Americans went to Oregon for a new start. These pioneers traveled along the Oregon Trail in covered wagons. The Oregon Trail started in Missouri and ended in Oregon. This was the best way to cross the Rocky Mountains. The trip along the trail was very hard, and it took four to eight months to reach the end. Many pioneers died along the way. Once those who made it reached Oregon, many of them built new homes, farms, and towns.

Oregon became a U.S. **territory** in 1848. More settlers arrived when gold was discovered in nearby California and then in Oregon. Oregon became the thirty-third state on February 14, 1859.

This painting shows pioneers in a wagon train making their way into Oregon. A wagon train is a long line of wagons traveling across the country.

Mountains and Rain

Oregon is known for its foggy, rainy coast. However, the state has many other features, too. The beautiful Cascade Mountain Range is in western Oregon, and the dry Harney Basin is in east central Oregon. The eastern part of the state also has the Columbia Plateau.

The highest point in Oregon is Mount Hood. Part of the Cascade Range, Mount Hood is one of the most-climbed mountains in the world. It has 12 **glaciers**, and snow covers its top all year long.

Western Oregon is cool and rainy because the mountains hold the wet air from the Pacific Ocean over the area. This area has many winter storms, which can create strong winds and 20-foot- (6 m) high waves! Eastern Oregon is drier.

Shown here is Mount Hood, in northern Oregon. Mount Hood is 11,249 feet (3,429 m) tall.

Sea Lions, Beavers, and Wildflowers

There are many different plants and animals in Oregon. Sea lions live on the coast, and salmon and bass swim in Oregon's rivers. Bald eagles can be found in Oregon, and the northern spotted owl can be found there, too. Because northern spotted owls are **endangered**, many forests in Oregon have been closed to logging so that the owls have places to live. The state is nicknamed the Beaver State because of the large number of beavers that settlers once trapped for fur there.

Oregon's forests are rich in Douglas fir and ponderosa pine trees. Many kinds of wildflowers grow in the Columbia River Gorge. The Columbia Plateau has many grasslands.

Here you can see a group of Steller sea lions on Oregon's coast. When they are not catching fish, Steller sea lions spend time on the state's rocky shores.

What Comes from Oregon?

Oregon is known for its trees. The state is one of the largest producers of **timber** in the country. Timber is shipped to other parts of Oregon and to other states, where it is used to make wood products, such as paper and plywood. Too many trees have been cut down throughout the state, though. There are concerns that cutting trees down can be harmful to the environment. Because of this, the timber business in Oregon is getting smaller.

Oregon produces other goods, though. Miners there dig for gemstones and gold. Factories make computers and electronic **equipment**. Oregon has many farms that grow everything from Christmas trees and peppermint to wheat. Other farms produce dairy products and raise cattle for beef.

Many different tools and machinery are used in the timber business. Here a man is shown using a log loader to stack timber in Washington County, Oregon.

Seeing Salem and Portland

Oregon's two biggest cities are Salem and Portland. Salem, the state capital, is one of the oldest communities in the state. The city is nicknamed the Cherry City because of the many cherry orchards, or cherry farms, that were once in the area.

Portland is Oregon's largest city. More than 530,000 people live there. There are many interesting things to do in Portland. Tom McCall Waterfront Park has restaurants and river walks. Kids can go to the Oregon Museum of Science and Industry and visit the **planetarium** there. Grant Park has **sculptures** of characters from books by Beverly Cleary. Cleary is a famous children's book author who once lived in Portland.

Here you can see downtown Portland and Tom McCall Waterfront Park, along the Willamette River. This park is a popular place to walk and hear music.

A Volcano Makes a Lake

Did you know that the deepest lake in the United States was made by a volcano? Crater Lake, in southwest Oregon, was created over 7,700 years ago when Mount Mazama, a volcano, **erupted** and **collapsed**. The collapse created a deep basin called a caldera, which then filled with water. Crater Lake is 1,943 feet (592 m) deep. It is surrounded by tall cliffs and has two islands. There are no streams to bring water into Crater Lake or take it away. Instead, the lake fills with water from melting winter snow. **Evaporation** keeps the lake from overflowing.

Crater Lake is inside Crater Lake National Park. The park is found in southern Oregon. It is 100 miles (160 km) east of the Pacific Ocean.

Crater Lake, shown here, gets around 533 inches (1,354 cm) of snow each year. All together, that snow would reach higher than a four-story building!

Come to Oregon

Oregon has something for everyone. Visitors can see Multnomah Falls, near Troutdale, which are 620 feet (189 m) high. Near Florence, they can view sea lions at Sea Lion Caves, where an elevator takes visitors down into one of the world's largest sea caves. History lovers can visit a **reconstruction** of Lewis and Clark's Fort Clatsop, on the coast of Oregon near the border with Washington. At the Evergreen Aviation Museum, in McMinnville, you can see the *Spruce Goose*, a famous plane from the 1940s.

Whether you like the city, the country, or history, Oregon has something for you. That is one of the reasons why so many people are proud to call this state their home.

Glossary

collapsed (kuh-LAPSD) Fell down suddenly.

endangered (in-DAYN-jerd) In danger of no longer living.

equipment (uh-KWIP-mint) All the supplies needed to do something.

erupted (ih-RUPT-ed) To have had a volcano send up gases, smoke, or lava.

evaporation (ih-va-puh-RAY-shun) When a liquid, like water, changes to a gas.

explorers (ek-SPLOR-erz) People who travel and look for new land.

glaciers (GLAY-shurz) Large masses of ice that move down a mountain or along a valley.

logging (LOG-ing) The act or business of cutting down trees.

pioneers (py-uh-NEERZ) Some of the first people to settle in a new area.

planetarium (pla-nih-TER-ee-um) A theater with a domed screen on top used for looking at pictures of the night sky.

reconstruction (ree-kun-STRUKT-shun) A replica, or copy, of a building that used to exist.

sculptures (SKULP-cherz) Figures that are shaped or formed.

territory (TER-uh-tor-ee) Land that is controlled by a person or a group of people.

timber (TIM-bur) Wood that is cut and used for building.

tribes (TRYBZ) Groups of people who share the same way of life and relatives.

Oregon State Symbols

State Tree
Douglas Fir

State Animal
Beaver

State Flag
Front

State Flag
Back

State Bird
Western
Meadowlark

State Flower
Oregon Grape

State Seal

Famous People from Oregon

Chief Joseph
(1840–1904)
Born in Wallowa Valley, OR
Native American Leader

Beverly Cleary
(1916–)
Born in McMinnville, OR
Author

Matt Groening
(1954–)
Born in Portland, OR
Cartoonist

Oregon State Map

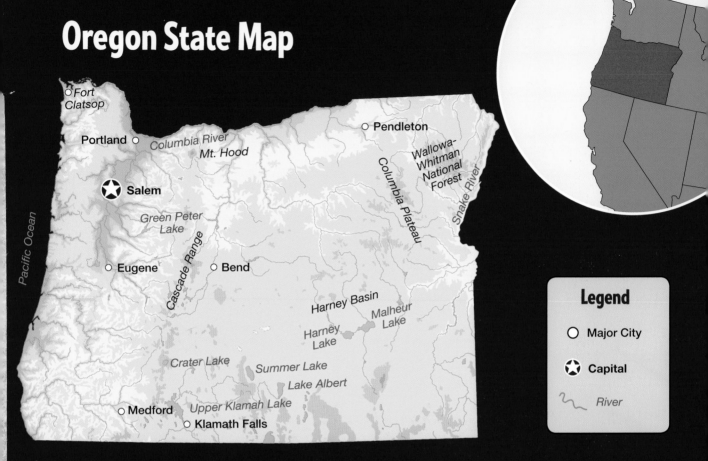

Fort Clatsop

Portland

Columbia River

Mt. Hood

Pendleton

Wallowa-Whitman National Forest

Columbia Plateau

Snake River

Salem

Green Peter Lake

Cascade Range

Pacific Ocean

Eugene

Bend

Harney Basin

Malheur Lake

Harney Lake

Crater Lake

Summer Lake

Lake Albert

Medford

Upper Klamah Lake

Klamath Falls

Legend

○ Major City

✪ Capital

～ River

Oregon State Facts

Population: About 3,421,437

Area: 97,073 square miles (251,418 sq km)

Motto: "She flies with her own wings"

Song: "Oregon, My Oregon," words by John A. Buchanan, music by Henry B. Murtagh

Index

Web Sites

Due to the changing nature of Internet links, PowerKids Press has developed an online list of Web sites related to the subject of this book. This site is updated regularly. Please use this link to access the list:

www.powerkidslinks.com/amst/or/